ANTI-RACISM STARTS WITH FAMILY

Note for parents,

Help your younger children to read and to explain the messages of hope and understanding. Its an opportunity to educate anti-racism with your family.

The back page of each coloring page is blank to prevent ink bleed into the next illustration.

' IT'S NOT ENOUGH TO BE NON-RACIST. WE MUST BE ANTI-RACIST '

We are All Equal.
We came here by
Birth and will
leave in Death

Love Sees
No Color

Don't Be
Divided
Stay United

Racism and
Hate have
No Place
Here

Skin Color is Not Reasonable Suspicion

We are More
Powerful
When we
Empower Each
Other

Race does
Not
Biologically
Exist

Different Color does not mean different human

There is one
race.
the
humanity

The only Thing that should Be Separated by Color is laundry

solidarity
forever

We All
Blade the
Same Color

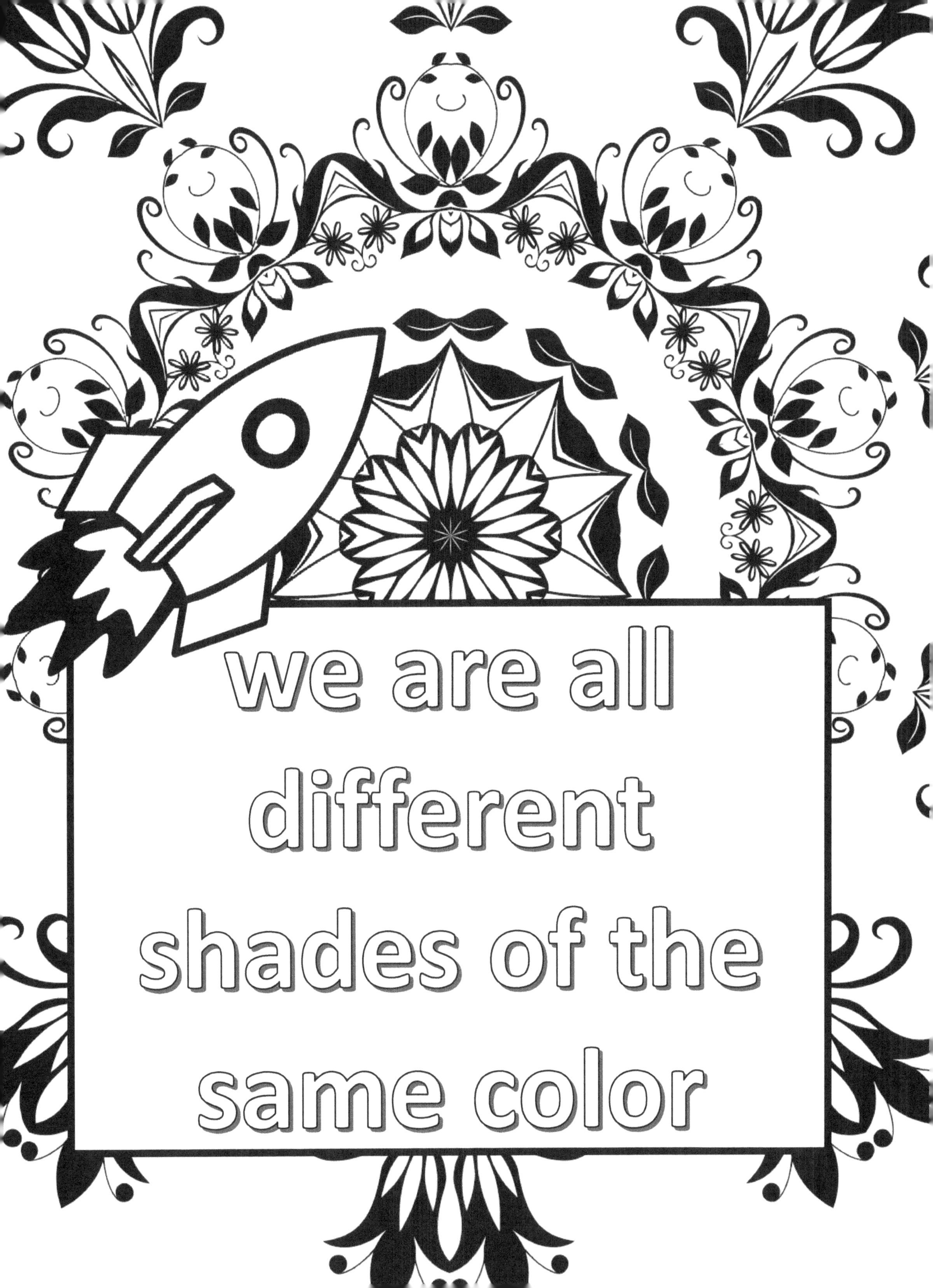

we are all
different
shades of the
same color

It's not enough
To Be Non-
Racist.
We must Be
Anti-Racist

All colors
are
beautiful

Take a Hand
against
Racism

Judging a Person does not Define Who They are.
It defines Who You are

Stop
Racist
Ideas

Your Opinion
of Me doesn't
Define Who
I am

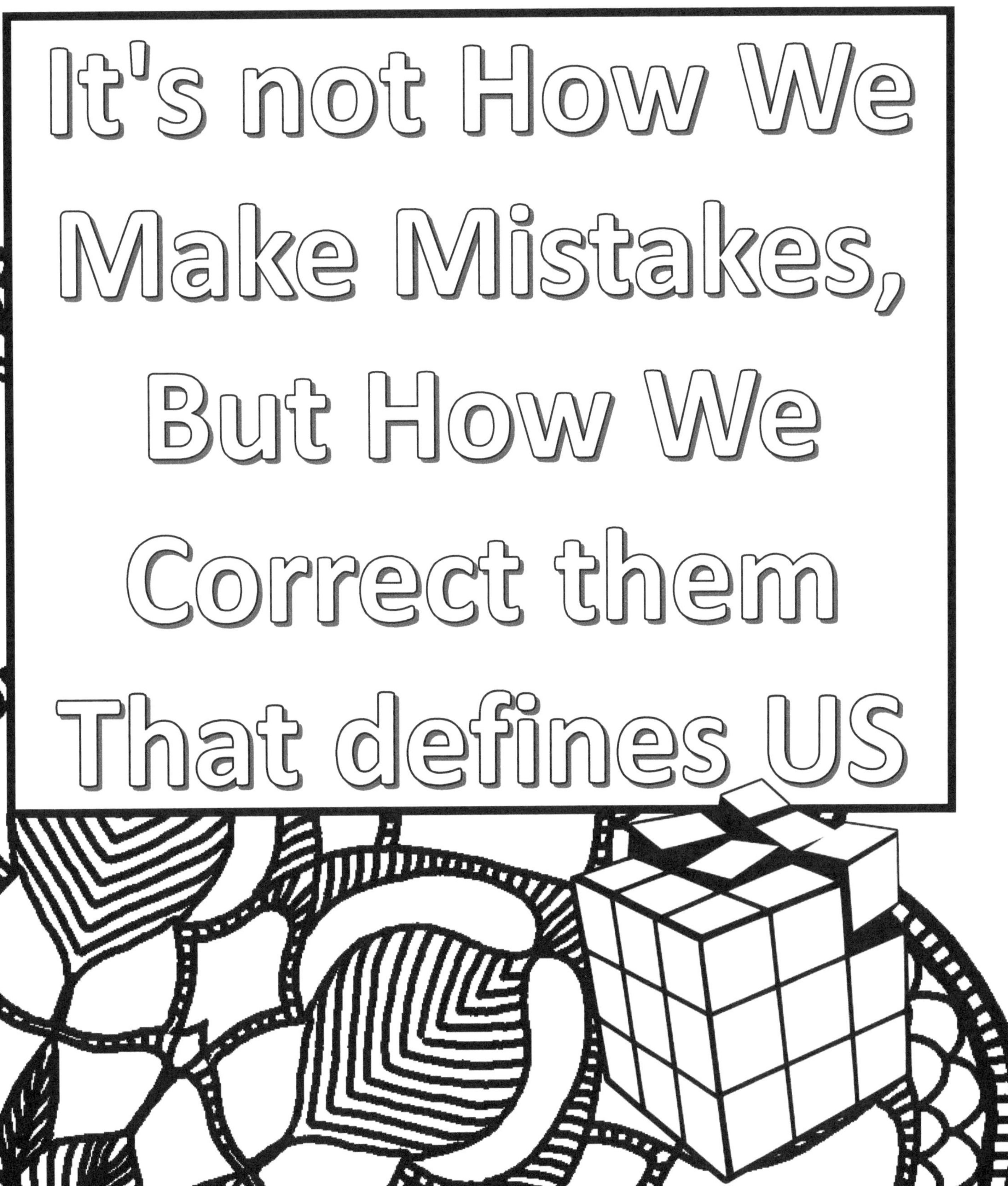

It's not How We
Make Mistakes,
But How We
Correct them
That defines US

Privilege is invisible To Those Who are Born With it

Don't Judge Me By my Color. If You do, You will Miss Entirely Who I am

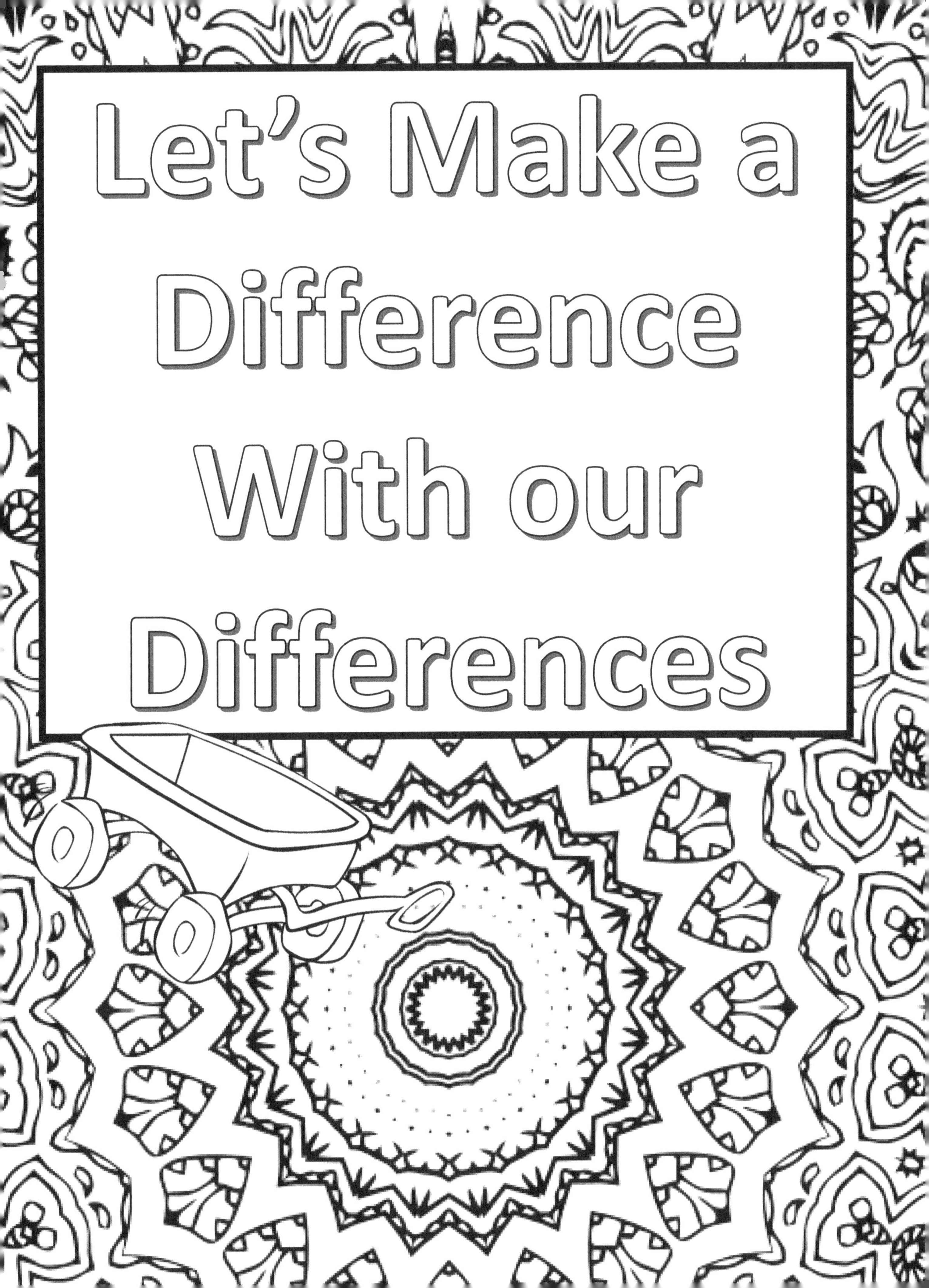

Let's Make a
Difference
With our
Differences

Color
is Not a
Crime

Hate causes a lot of Problems - But Hasn't Solved One

Stronger
People
Stand Up
For Others

Don't Judge
Someone just
Because They
Sin Differently
Than You

People of Quality Do not Fear Equality

We can't Change What People say, But We Can change How we React

School Bus
begin each
day with a
grateful heart